The Heavenly Gift

Studies in the Work of the Holy Spirit

By

MYER PEARLMAN

Published by
Gospel Publishing House
Springfield, Mo.

CHAPTER I

THE LIFE OF THE SPIRIT AND THE NEED OF TODAY

The doctrine of the Holy Spirit, judged by the place it occupies in the Scriptures, stands in the foremost rank of redemptive truths. With the exception of 2 and 3 John, every book in the New Testament contains a reference to the Spirit's work; every Gospel begins with a promise of His effusion. There can be no doubt about the importance of the Holy Spirit in the early church, for in those days a person was not considered a genuine disciple unless he was indwelt by the Spirit. "Now if any man have not the Spirit of Christ, he is none of his." Rom. 8:9. (Note: That the words "Spirit of Christ" refer to the Holy Spirit is indicated by the context and proved by 1 Peter 1:10, where the expression "Spirit of Christ" can refer only to the Holy Spirit. The Holy Spirit is called the "Spirit of Christ" because He is sent in Christ's *name* (John 14:26), and because His ministry is to make real in believers the redemptive work of Christ.) One of the accusations brought by Jude against certain false teachers of his day was expressed in the phrase, "having not the Spirit." Jude 19. In the early days of Christianity, to say that a person was a Christian was to imply that he had the Holy Spirit.

There can be no vital Christianity apart from the Holy Spirit. "Wherever Christianity has become a living power," writes Dr. Smeaton, "the doctrine of the Holy Spirit has uniformly been regarded equally with the atonement and justification by faith as an article of a standing or a falling church. The distinctive feature of Christianity as it addresses itself to man's experience is the work of the Holy Spirit, which elevates it not only far above all philosophical speculations but also above every other form of religion." We are reminded by this quotation that there are two sides to Christianity: the *outward,* consisting of the work of the Lord Jesus Christ—His ministry, death, resurrection and ascension; and the *inward* side, represented by the operation of the Holy Spirit through whom facts are made real to us. The Spirit is sent to do *in* us what Christ has done *for* us. It is possible to have the external features of Christianity (important as these are) without possessing the reality.

An age-long problem of the church has been to make the religion of Jesus Christ so vivid and real as to grip the heart, awaken the conscience, and influence the lives of people. Now, there is a right way and a wrong way of making Christianity vivid. The wrong way is the way of ritualism, which endeavors to stir people's emotions by means of elaborate ceremonies, fragrant incense, artistic pictures, and impressive music. It is an appeal to the senses. The right way is to lead people into a personal spiritual experience which inspires and strengthens them for the conflict of life and the service of God. It is an appeal to the spirit of man. It is the New Testament way, the way of the Spirit. In these days of religious declension, people become discouraged because of the powerlessness and lack of authority of nominal Christianity. They are looking for reality in the religion of Jesus, and each of the above mentioned types of Christianity makes appeal to them. How important, then, for the Church to give honor to what has been the "neglected doctrine" of the Holy Spirit, and to recapture for herself and others what has been described as "the lost radiance of Christianity!"

Many years ago a godly minister surveyed the religious situation and cried in alarm, "We have unlearned the Holy Spirit!" Even a Catholic, Cardinal Manning, made the admission, "I have long thought that the secret but real cause of the so-called Reformation was that the office of the Holy Ghost has been much obscured in popular belief." The church has unlearned the Holy Spirit; but she must learn Him again if this age is to be gripped by the gospel.

Whether or not the fact is realized or recognized, the greatest need of the age in which we live is spiritual power. William G. Peck, after a survey of modern conditions, concludes that "we are living in what is probably one of the supreme crises in human history. The profoundest thought in the world now is persuaded that we have reached the end of our modern experiment. The spiritual springs of what we have called the modern world are exhausted. Its driving force is gone. The economic breakdown is but the outer symbol of a deep-seated collapse of the human spirit. And that is why those people who fondly imagine that we are experiencing no more than a trade slump are dangerously deceiving themselves. . . . The secular life of the modern world is falling to pieces because it has no purpose which can satisfy the inner life of man." He sounds a note of encouragement: "And let me declare to you who own the Christian name that never before has there been so vast an opportunity for the gospel in the world as the immediate future is going to present. So far from being obsolete, the Christian faith is the one solid and certain thing left standing in a world where other landmarks are rapidly being submerged. Believe me, all the little people who are running about, remarking that Christianity is played out, and that in the future men will have no need of religion, are themselves full of stale second-hand ideas. It is they who cannot read the signs of the times."

Many who have fondly hoped that the progress of scientific thought would do away with the need of spiritual things have been disappointed. Another confirmation to our faith in the efficacy of the old-time power of the gospel is supplied by the following editorial which appeared some years ago in the *New York Times,* under the heading "Indestructible Religion."

Never before, perhaps, have nations so much needed religion as a motive and sanction, and as food for faith, hope, and charity. "Pure reason" and the "naked truth" tell so little of the ends of existence. They accompany the human spirit a little way along the road, but cannot tell where the road of human life began or whither it leads or just why the journey was begun. The ideal dwells in the region just beyond the present hearing or seeing of science, and is reached only when faith leads on through the encircling gloom and furnishes the one goal that satisfies the soul of man.

Man must ever rectify his faith by the truth that science brings. He must continue to penetrate the mystery about him. But he must continue to adore the mystery that still remains, for when that adoration ceases and the mind's desire fails, the life of the world shrinks to the visible and audible and the palpable whose walls are tomb.

Religion will not let a man be content with such a fate. Its efficacy is that it carries into the realms beyond. Nothing is so much needed today in the rehabilitation of the broken world as a faith that still holds toward a higher, diviner goal than mere social and economic and political adjustment—than things that are purely physical and temporal.

It is therefore evident that the great discovery this poor world needs belongs to a realm higher than the scientific. The late Charles P. Steinmetz, a great scientist in the realm of electricity, made the following significant statement: "I think that the greatest discovery will be along spiritual lines. Here is a force which history clearly shows has been the greatest power in the development of men and history, and yet we have been merely playing with it and have never seriously studied it as we have the physical forces. Some day people will learn that material things do not bring happiness, and are of little use in making men and women creative and powerful. Then the scientists of the world will turn their laboratories over to the study of

God, of prayer, and the spiritual forces which as yet have hardly been scratched. When that day comes the world will see more advancement in one generation than it has seen in the past four."

However, scientists, unaided, are not equipped to study "the spiritual forces which as yet have hardly been scratched," for Jesus described the Spirit as the One "whom the world cannot receive, because it seeth him not, neither knoweth him." John 14:17. He also added, "But ye know him." Therefore, those who know Him in a measure are equipped for the study of His operations in human nature and the laws governing those workings.

The studies that follow are offered as a slight help to the understanding of the Holy Spirit. It will be noticed that they are largely explanatory in character, being designed as a foundation for teaching the practical aspects of the spiritual life. Inasmuch as the experimental side of the Spirit's work has been splendidly emphasized among us, a doctrinal presentation of the subject may prove helpful.

May we approach our study with the prayer expressed in that ancient hymn, *Veni Creator.*

> Creator, Spirit! by whose aid
> The world's foundations first were laid,
> Come, visit every pious mind,
> Come, pour Thy joys on humankind:
> From sin and sorrow set us free,
> And make Thy temples worthy Thee.
>
> O Source of uncreated light,
> The Father's promised Paraclete!
> Thrice holy Fount, thrice holy Fire,
> Our hearts with heavenly love inspire:
> Come, and Thy sacred unction bring,
> To sanctify us while we sing.

Plenteous of grace, descend from high,
Rich in Thy sevenfold energy!
Thou Strength of His almighty hand,
Whose power does heaven and earth command,
Refine and purge our earthly parts,
But oh inflame and fire our hearts!

CHAPTER II

THE HOLY SPIRIT IN THE OLD TESTAMENT

The Holy Spirit is revealed in the Old Testament in three ways: first, as the cosmic or creative Spirit, through whose power the universe and all living creatures were created; second, as the dynamic or power-giving Spirit; third, as the redemptive Spirit, or the Holy Spirit by whom human nature is changed.

Let us consider the three operations of the Spirit—creative, dynamic, redemptive.

I. CREATIVE.

The Holy Spirit is the third Person of the Godhead, and the One by whose power the universe was created. "And the spirit of God moved upon the face of the waters." Gen. 1:2. "By his spirit he hath garnished the heavens." Job 26:13. "By the word of the Lord were the heavens made; and all the host of them by the breath of his mouth." Psalm 33:6. "Thou sendest forth thy spirit, they are created; and thou renewest the face of the earth." Psalm 104:30. The physical universe, with all its powers, laws, and beauties, is the work of the Holy Spirit. Moreover, the same Holy Spirit who created the physical world on the outside, creates a new world *within us,* by regeneration.

Now the same Holy Spirit by whose power the universe was created, also created man. We read that "the Lord God formed man of the dust of the ground, and breathed into his nostrils the breath of life; and man became a living soul." Gen. 2:7. "The spirit of God hath made me, and the breath of the Almighty hath given me life." Job 33:4. Every person in this world experiences daily the indwelling of the Holy Spirit, in the creative sense. That is, every person is sustain-

11

ed by the creative power of God's Spirit. Daniel describes Belshazzar's relationship to God, as follows: "In whose hand thy breath is, and whose are all thy ways." Dan. 5:23.   Paul said, "For in him we live, and move, and have our being." Acts 17:28. This relationship to God reveals the meaning of sin. What is sin? Fundamentally, it is the perversion, or abuse, of God-given powers and faculties, so that every time a person commits sin he uses the power of the Creator to outrage Him. But observe that although God is in every man in the creative sense, yet He does not *dwell* in every man; God *is* everywhere, but does not *dwell* everywhere. When God *dwells* in a person, He enters into a loving, personal, and internal relationship with him. This we call the indwelling of the Holy Spirit.

II. DYNAMIC.

The Spirit of God, as the creative Spirit creates the world, and creates man in order that he may form a society governed by God's laws; in other words, the kingdom of God. In opposition to the kingdom of God is the "world," or human society organized apart from the laws of God. (We shall discover that human society organized *apart* from God ultimately becomes human society organized *against* God.)

After sin had entered the world and spiritual darkness covered the earth, God made a new start by calling Israel, organizing them under His law, and so constituting them the kingdom of Jehovah. 2 Chron. 13:8. As we study the history of Israel, we read of the Holy Spirit's inspiring certain individuals in Israel, to rule and to guide the members of that kingdom, and to supervise their progress in the life of consecration to Jehovah.

Now in studying the power-giving manifestations of the Holy Ghost in Israel, we shall find that the Holy Spirit produces two kinds of ministries: first, *doers for God*—men of action, organizers, executives; second, *speakers for God*—prophets and teachers. A moment's thought will convince us that both classes are needed in the church today—workers for God and speakers for God—provided they are energized by the Spirit of God. We read that Moses was mighty in *"words and deeds."* Acts 7:22. We read also that Jesus "began both to *do* and *teach."* Acts 1:1.

Doers for God

In Ex. 31:2, 3 we read these words: "See, I have called by name Bezaleel the son of Uri, the son of Hur, of the tribe of Judah: and I have filled him with the Spirit of God, in wisdom, and in understanding, and in knowledge, and in all manner of workmanship." Moses had the blueprints and specifications for the Tabernacle, but an expert was needed who could understand those blueprints and specifications and erect the building.

The same need exists today. In the New Testament we have the blueprints for the building of the church of Jesus Christ, but Spirit-energized executives are needed to put these plans into operation. Perhaps you have met persons who say they do not believe in any organization. What such persons really mean is that they have no use for *abuses* of organization. It must be sadly confessed that organization *has* been frightfully abused. Read Acts 6:1-5. The membership of the early church increased so rapidly that the administration of its affairs became difficult. The widows of the Greek-speaking Jews were neglected in the "relief work," and there was danger of a division in the church between the Greek-speaking Jews and the Hebrew-speaking Jews. How was the trouble settled? By adding more organization. Seven men were chosen to assume charge of the financial affairs of the church. But notice one qualification insisted upon: they had to be men "full of the Holy Ghost and wisdom." The apostles may have reasoned that if the leaders and the workers on the tabernacle needed the Spirit of God, how much more do the workers in the spiritual building of the church need to be filled with the Spirit of God? And this is the New Testament qualification for every deacon—that he should be filled with the Holy Ghost.

The insistence that even administrators of the secular affairs of the church should be Spirit-filled reminds us of the fact that the primitive Christians knew by real experience the indwelling of the Holy Ghost in the church. The Spirit of God was so real among them that He gave a peculiar power and a peculiar touch to everything they did and to everything they said. And do you know why certain churches teach that when one is baptized in water he is born again? that when one takes the elements of the Lord's Supper he is partaking of the real body and blood of the Lord Jesus Christ? that when the bishop lays his hands upon people they receive the Holy Ghost? Personally I believe it is a testimony to the fact that in the early days of Christianity the Holy Ghost was so real and gave such wonderful power to the ministries of the church, that in the baptismal service and in the communion service the power of God was really manifest; and when the apostles laid hands on people and prayed for them, they *did* receive the Holy Spirit. It seems to me this is what happened in the early church. When the inspiration of the Spirit had left the church, people began to reason in this way: "The power of God used to be manifestly present at the baptismal services. Perhaps there is power connected with baptismal water. In that case, to be baptized in water is to be born again. The power of God used to be manifest in the communion service. Perhaps the power inheres in the elements, so that when one receives the elements he receives the actual body and blood of Christ, His real Deity. And when the apostles laid hands upon people and they received the Holy Ghost, it must have been the laying on of hands that brought power. Well, we will lay hands upon people, repeat a formula, and they will receive the Holy Ghost."

Now, formal and dead and lifeless as all this ritualism is, it is a sad testimony to the fact that away back yonder the Holy Ghost was so real in the church that He gave a peculiar power to everything said and done; so that it was expected that even the men who handled the financial affairs should be full of the Holy Ghost.

There came a time when Moses lost patience with his congregation of about two million people. He had two tasks: first, to get *Israel out of Egypt;* and second, to get *Egypt out of Israel,* and the second seemed to be the more difficult of the two. The time came when the congregation tried his patience. Numbers 11. When they began murmuring for flesh Moses could stand it no longer. Imagine him crying, "My ministry is a failure! I have brought them out of Egypt, and listen to their murmuring for the fleshpots of Egypt. I wish I were dead!" What did God do? He said, in effect, to Moses, "What you need is some help. I am going to give you a *board of deacons* of seventy men, and I will take some of the power that is upon you and put it upon those men, that they may minister." This incident may suggest another reason why the apostles insisted that those seven men who administered the affairs of the church must be filled with the Holy Spirit.

Under the heading "Doers for God" we should not forget to mention the Judges of Israel, those men of action energized by the Spirit of Jehovah to deliver Israel from their enemies and to govern the people of Jehovah.

Speakers for God

A simple and brief way of describing an Old Testament prophet is to call him a "speaker for God"—a man who received a message from God and spoke it forth to the people. In this section we shall compare the prophetic experience with the New Testament experience known as the Baptism with the Holy Spirit. The comparison is legitimate, for the prophetic enduement was given for the purpose of empowering people to speak for God. Compare Acts 1:8.

There are three points of resemblance between the prophetic enduement and the New Testament enduement.

1. The Old Testament prophet was conscious of a supernatural power coming upon him from time to time, enabling him to utter messages not conceived in his own mind. In order to be a priest one had to measure up to certain qualifications: he had to be physically perfect, he had to belong to the tribe of Levi, and be of the male sex. But there was only one qualification necessary to make a man or woman or child a prophet, and that was that the Spirit of Jehovah should rest upon him or her. One could always know what a priest was going to do, because he would work according to the ritual; but it was difficult to foresee what a prophet was going to do or say, for he represented the free movings of God's Spirit. The priesthood represented the organized and established religion, and the daily routine of pastoral work; the prophets of the Old Testament represented the evangelistic ministry.

The very word "prophet" is suggestive of inspiration. It is translated from a word which means "to bubble up." Why was he given such a name? The priest taught the law, and his expositions were rather dry and uninspiring; but when the prophet spoke in the name of Jehovah, the words just rolled out of him in torrents; people listening to him probably said, "That man's words bubble up like a spring."

2. The second resemblance between the prophetic and the Pentecostal experiences is indicated by the expressions used in both cases. In referring to the origin of their power, the prophets said that God poured out the Spirit, gave the Spirit, put His Spirit upon them, filled them with His Spirit, and put His Spirit within. Describing the variety of influence, they declared that the Spirit was on them, rested upon them, laid hold of

them. To indicate the influence exerted on them, they
said they were filled with the Spirit, moved by the
Spirit, taken up by the Spirit, and that the Spirit spoke
through them. All these expressions denote the suddenness and supernatural nature of the power that came
upon them, and they are similar to the expressions used
to describe the New Testament Baptism with the Holy
Ghost.

These expressions convey the truth that the
prophet in the Old Testament did not use the Holy
Ghost—the Holy Ghost used him. He could not
prophesy when he wanted to, neither could he use the
gift at will. He had to wait for the prophetic inspiration. Now there are some who say, "I have heard of
people who say they can speak with other tongues at
will." I disbelieve that claim. To *really* speak with
other tongues, one must be inspired by the Spirit of
God; we cannot use the Spirit of God. We do not
need more of the Holy Ghost: *we need to let the Holy
Ghost have more of us!*

3. Another respect in which the experience of the
prophet resembles the Baptism with the Holy Ghost is
in the fact that when the prophet prophesied, he was
sometimes in an exalted condition known as ecstasy.
What is ecstasy? It is a more dignified form of the
old expression "under the power," that state of being
in which one is lifted above ordinary consciousness and
into the spiritual realm, the realm of prophecy. Ezekiel
said, "The hand of the Lord God (the power of the
Lord God) fell there upon me, . . . and the spirit
lifted me up between the earth and the heaven, and
brought me in the visions of God to Jerusalem." Ezek.
8:1-3. It is very likely that Isaiah was in such a condition when he beheld the glory of Jehovah. Isaiah 6.
John the apostle says that he was "in the Spirit on the
Lord's day." Rev. 1:10. "While I prayed in the temple,
I was in a trance (ecstasy)," testifies Paul. Acts 22:17.
When people experience the Baptism with the Holy

Ghost as it is described in the book of Acts, the supernatural utterance that accompanies this experience is an evidence of an ecstatic condition. Some time ago a young man wrote asking me the following question: "Is the Baptism with tongues the only baptism? May not one have a mighty filling and be given power for service without the tongues?" As I remember it, this was part of my answer: "The Baptism with the Holy Ghost is an experience in which the Spirit of God makes such a direct and powerful impact upon the spirit of man that a condition of ecstasy results, and in that ecstatic condition a person speaks ecstatically, in a language he has never learned." I suggested that if the Spirit of God made the same impact upon his spirit that He made on the disciples, he would experience the same ecstatic condition and that the same ecstatic utterance would follow.

III. REDEMPTIVE.

The Holy Spirit in the Old Testament is also revealed as the redemptive Spirit, or the Spirit that transforms human nature according to the image of God; however this operation is referred to more often as a future event than as a present experience. The expression *"Holy* Spirit"* is used only twice in the Old Testament, but eighty-eight times in the New Testament. What is the significance of this fact? It is that in the Old Testament the emphasis is upon the operation of the Spirit as a dynamic power, while in the New Testament the emphasis is upon the operation of the Spirit as a redemptive or sanctifying power.

In the Old Testament the Spirit of God is never referred to by the brief designation, "the Spirit." One always reads of "the Spirit of Jehovah" or "the Spirit of God." But in the New Testament the brief title "the Spirit," is of very frequent occurrence. To illustrate: I am introduced to a stranger whom I address as Mr. Johnson. After several months I begin to greet him as "John." What has occurred? Through frequent intercourse I have become acquainted with him. Now, the fact that the Spirit of God in the New Testament is described so often by the brief designation "the Spirit," suggests that His operations are no longer isolated manifestations, but familiar occurrences.

The Old Testament prophets looked forward to the time when the Holy Ghost would be poured out upon mankind in a way they had never experienced. They told of the time when Jehovah would cleanse the hearts of the people, put His Spirit within them, and write His law in their inward parts. Ezek. 36:25-29. God speaking through Joel (2:28) declared: "And it shall come to pass afterward, that I will pour out my spirit upon all flesh; and your sons and your daughters shall prophesy, your old men shall dream dreams, your young men shall see visions." For what purpose? To lead people back to God, for we read in verse 32, "And it shall come to pass, that whosoever shall call on the name of the Lord shall be delivered." The prophets also spoke of a great Person upon whom the Spirit of Jehovah was to abide in extraordinary fullness. That Person was the Messiah, or "Anointed One."

What is the connection between these two great events of prophecy—the coming of the Anointed One, and the universal outpouring of the Holy Ghost? John the Baptist answers: "I indeed baptize you with water unto repentance: but he that cometh after me is mightier than I, whose shoes I am not worthy to bear: *he shall baptize you with the Holy Ghost,* and with fire." In other words, the Messiah is the Giver of the Holy Spirit, and this is the subject of our next study.

CHAPTER III

THE GIVER AND GIFT OF THE SPIRIT

The foundation for the doctrine of the Holy Spirit is found in the account of man's creation. Many scholars believe that when God created man and breathed into his nostrils the breath of life, He imparted not only mental and physical life but also the Holy Spirit. That sounds plausible enough, for since Adam was created perfect, he must have been created with the Holy Spirit, without which our personality is not complete. When our first parents sinned, spiritual death began, and they lost the indwelling Spirit. Therefore when the Redeemer came, His mission was to restore the Holy Spirit to mankind. "Christ hath redeemed us from the curse of the law, being made a curse for us; for it is written, Cursed is every one that hangeth on a tree: that the blessing of Abraham might come on the Gentiles through Jesus Christ; *that we might receive the promise of the Spirit* through faith." Gal. 3:13, 14.

As we learned in our last study, the Old Testament prophets foretold a mighty effusion of God's Spirit in the latter days, this effusion being connected with the ministry of an individual endowed with the Spirit of Jehovah in extraordinary measure, and because of that anointing called the Messiah, or "Anointed One." Considering these predictions in the light of the New Testament we come to the following conclusion: the great blessing of the Messianic Age is the outpouring of the Spirit, and it is the prerogative of the Messiah to impart the Spirit to individuals. In this study we shall consider: first, the *Giver;* and second, the *Gift* He imparts.

I. THE GIVER

From the beginning to the end of His earthly life,

the Lord Jesus Christ was intimately connected with the Holy Spirit. So close is the connection between our Lord and the Spirit of God that the apostle Paul declares, "The first man Adam was made a living soul; the last Adam was made a quickening spirit." 1 Cor. 15:45. (Not that Jesus *is* the Holy Spirit, but that He imparts the Spirit.) He was conceived by the Holy Spirit and had the witness of the Spirit that He was the Son of God. Luke 2:49. Then at the age of thirty He received the enduement of the Holy Spirit, so that officially He became the Messiah, the "Anointed One," upon whom dwells without measure the Spirit of the living God. And John says, "He that sent me to baptize with water, the same said unto me, Upon whom thou shalt see the Spirit descending, and *remaining* on him, the same is he who baptizeth with the Holy Ghost." John 1:33. The anointing that came upon the Lord Jesus at the river Jordan was, unlike our enduement, an anointing without measure. John 3:34. It was also a *permanent* anointing; as we shall see that it never left Him and is with Him this day.

Let us continue the thought. After being led of the Spirit to defeat Satan in the wilderness, Christ ministered in the power of that Spirit. Peter tells "how God anointed Jesus of Nazareth with the Holy Ghost and with power: who went about doing good, and healing all that were oppressed of the devil; for God was with him." Acts 10:38. When Jesus came into the synagogue, He said, "The Spirit of the Lord is upon me, because he hath anointed me." Luke 4:18. By that same Spirit He was given power to go to the cross and die for the sins of mankind; He was the One "who through the eternal Spirit offered himself without spot to God." Heb. 9:14. In other words, when He went to the cross, the anointing of the Spirit was upon Him. By that same Spirit He was raised from the dead. Rom. 1:4. After the resurrection, with the Messianic anointing still upon Him, He appeared unto His disciples, breathed upon them, and said, "Receive ye the

Holy Ghost." John 20:19-22. (We are not ignorant of the fact that many well-known Bible teachers believe that this was an exhortation or command to tarry and be filled, directions which He repeated later as recorded in Luke 24:49. However, we consider, in agreement with other well-known Bible scholars, that at this time He imparted to the ones on whom He breathed, a fore-taste of Pentecost.) During the forty days between His resurrection and ascension—the anointing still upon Him—He was taken up, "after that he through the Holy Ghost had given commandments unto the apostles whom he had chosen." Acts 1:2. On the day of Pentecost those one hundred and twenty realized by personal experience that the Lord Jesus Christ was the Baptizer with the Holy Ghost and with power. A little later Peter faced a curious crowd and said, "Therefore being by the right hand of God exalted, and having received of the Father the promise of the Holy Ghost, he hath shed forth this, which ye now see and hear." And today that same unlimited anointing abides upon Him, by which He is able to baptize with the Holy Ghost. Rev. 5:6.

Thus we see that the New Testament gives prominence to the truth that Jesus is the Giver of life because He is the Giver of the Spirit. He came into the world to break the power of sin and to make available for mankind a new source of spiritual life and power.

II. THE GIFT

Now that we have noticed the Giver, let us consider the nature of the Gift He offers to mankind. John 7:38, 39, "He that believeth on me, as the scripture hath said, out of His innermost being shall flow rivers of living water. (But this spake he of the Spirit, which they that believe on him should receive: for the Holy Ghost was not yet given; because that Jesus was not yet glorified.)" Note especially these words: "The Holy Ghost was not yet given; because that Jesus was not yet glorified." Did not the Holy Spirit come upon Moses, upon the Prophets, upon David, and upon many Old Testament leaders? How then can John say that "the Holy Ghost was *not yet given;* because that Jesus was not yet glorified"?

Was the Son of God in heaven, and was He manifested in some way to the world before He was born in a manger? See John 1:3. The answer is, Yes; but when He became incarnate, He entered the world *in a new way,* to sustain a new relationship to mankind. And He was given a new name, the name of Jesus. In like manner, the Holy Ghost was in the world, inspiring people before the day of Pentecost; but after the ascension of Jesus, the Holy Ghost came into the world *in a new way,* as the Spirit of the living Christ —that Spirit connected with that Person who suffered, died, rose again, and ascended. He was given a new name—the "Comforter."

Again, the meaning of John's words becomes clear when we consider that the emphasis is upon the word "given." The Holy Ghost was not yet a *gift* that could be the permanent possession of the individual. The following illustration was suggested to me by a friend. Let us suppose that you come to my home and ask to borrow my lawnmower. I say, "Help yourself." You take it, use it, and return it to me with a "Thank you." A week passes. Again you ask to borrow my lawnmower. I answer, "Help yourself." You use it and again return it with a "Thank you." This occurs many times. Finally I decide to get a new one. The next time you ask, "May I borrow your lawnmower?" I reply, "You may keep it. It is yours. It shall abide with you *always!*"

In Old Testament times God "lent," as it were, His Holy Spirit to people in the sense that the operation of the Holy Spirit was intermittent; He came upon people to endow them for some special service and then left them, to come upon them again on some other occasion. But after the day of Pentecost, Christ imparted the Holy Ghost as a permanent gift to be possessed and enjoyed. "He shall abide with you *for ever.*" I used to wonder what would happen to the indwelling Holy Spirit when we died. The answer is stated in John 4:14: "The water that I shall give him shall be in him a well of water springing up into *everlasting life.*" The Spirit comes from heaven, enters into us, and becomes to us the beginning of life eternal.

The question has been asked: "What is meant by the words in Acts 2:38, 'Ye shall receive the gift of the Holy Ghost'? Does it mean the Baptism with the Holy Ghost, or does it mean salvation?" I shall answer the question by asking questions. First: Do you believe that a person can be a really New Testament Christian without the Holy Spirit? The answer is, No. No person can be a really born-again New Testament Christian without the Holy Spirit. "If any man have not the Spirit of Christ (which is the Holy Spirit), he is none of his." Rom. 8:9. Second: Are there any truly born-again Christians outside our fellowship? The answer is, Yes. Therefore, there are people who have not experienced the Baptism with the Holy Spirit, but who possess, in a certain sense, the Holy Spirit. Third: Can the Holy Spirit come into a person to regenerate, give the witness of the Spirit, impart divine life, and bring Christ into his life—without dwelling within? The answer is, No; for all these operations imply, in some sense, an indwelling of the Holy Spirit.

When Peter said, "Repent, and be baptized every one of you in the name of Jesus Christ for the remission of sins, and ye shall receive the gift of the Holy Ghost," he was speaking of that gift in a general way. He might have said, "Repent of your sins, believe on the Lord Jesus Christ, and you will experience *the impartation of the Spirit.* You will receive Him in regenerating power; you will know Him in sanctifying power; He shall be yours in energizing power; more— He may see fit to impart a special gift (1 Cor. 12:7-10); and even more—from time to time you can ex-

perience new enduements and infillings." (Compare
Acts 2:4 and 4:31.)

In other words, I believe that the expression, "gift
of the Holy Spirit," is an inclusive one, comprising
every impartation of the Spirit of God given by the
Lord Jesus Christ. What do we mean by an inclusive
term? For example, the prophets spoke about Messiah's *coming;* but we know that there are really *two*
comings: first, in humiliation; second, in glory. We
speak about *the resurrection* from the dead; but we
really mean *two* resurrections: the resurrection of the
saints and the resurrection of the wicked. In like manner (in the writer's opinion), the "gift of the Holy
Spirit" may include many experiences with the Spirit.
In other words, it is a gift with many "packages." There
are many consecrated Christians who have received one
"package" of the gift of the Holy Spirit—His regenerating power. But there is another "package" known
as the Baptism with the Holy Spirit.

The inclusive nature of the Gift of the Spirit is
further illustrated in the Gospel according to John. In
the first twelve chapters of that book Jesus' teachings
on the Holy Spirit are addressed to the unconverted,
and the Spirit is presented as a life-giving power, dwelling within them, renewing them and issuing from them
as a refreshing stream. John 3:5-8; 4:10-13; 7:38-39.
According to chapter six, Jesus teaches that spiritual
life may be imparted only by eating the flesh and drink-
ing the blood of the Son of man. Though the Holy
Spirit is not directly mentioned, it is implied that this
impartation of life is effected by the Holy Spirit. John
6:63. The theme and purpose of Jesus' teachings on
the Holy Spirit in the first twelve chapters may be
summed up in the statement: "But as many as received
him, to them gave he power to become the sons of God,
even to them that believe on his name: which were
born, not of blood, nor of the will of the flesh, nor of
the will of man, but of God."

In chapters fourteen to sixteen we find that Jesus' teachings on the Spirit are addressed to His disciples. In these chapters the Holy Spirit is described, not as a regenerating power, but as an energizing power —as the "Comforter" sent to illumine and strengthen the disciples for future ministry. The theme of Jesus' teaching on the Spirit contained in these chapters is expressed in the Lord's own promise: "But ye shall receive power, after that the Holy Ghost is come upon you: and ye shall be witnesses unto me." Acts 1:8.

We admit that these two operations of the Holy Spirit are not differentiated in the Scriptures with mathematical precision; but there are general indications of the distinction; and that distinction has been confirmed by the experience of spiritual Christians in many churches, who teach and testify to the fact that in addition and subsequent to spiritual regeneration there is a baptism of power for Christians.

Let us now notice what constitutes the giving or the impartation of the Spirit of God. I believe it includes three experiences: first, the transformation of human nature (for salvation); second, the energizing of human nature (for service); third, the glorifying of human nature (for heaven).

I. THE TRANSFORMATION OF HUMAN NATURE.

First of all, the Spirit is given by Christ to regenerate or transform, human nature. I am not giving a theological definition of regeneration, because in most Pentecostal churches there are two pictures of regeneration. I refer to the two ordinances or sacraments, Water Baptism and Communion. These two sacraments, or ordinances, are pictures of the work of the Holy Ghost.

Some time ago, while walking down the street, I was accosted by a tired, dusty tramp who asked, "Where is the transient camp—the place where they put the hoboes?" He was then directed to the downtown transient hotel. As we know, a transient hotel is a

state institution where tired, dusty "hoboes" and others
may receive a bath, a meal, and a bed. What has all this
to do with the sacraments? Here is the explanation:
We are all transients ("pilgrims" the Bible calls us),
traveling from time to eternity, passing from one life
to another; the way is sometimes hard and we become
weary and defiled. Now, God sent Jesus Christ into
this world to establish a spiritual "transient hotel" for
spiritual transients, or pilgrims. I refer to the *church*,
the spiritual transient camp in which is found provision
for spiritual cleansing, spiritual food, and spiritual rest.
In other words, it is the ministry of the church to offer
these blessings to mankind. In order to set forth the
experiences preached by the church, the Lord Jesus has
instituted two ordinances, Water Baptism and Communion, which picture the work of the Holy Spirit.
Addressing His ministers, He as much as says: "I am
invisible to the world; but that the world may know who
I am and what I can do, I want you to do to the *bodies*
of the converts what I have done to their *souls*. When
I receive a person and bathe his *soul* in the living waters
of regeneration (Titus 3:4, 5), I want you to immerse
his *body* in baptismal waters, that the world may know
that I am the Regenerator. Also in order that mankind may know that I am the Sustainer of spiritual
life, I want you to eat bread and drink wine, in a sacred
meal, to commemorate My death—a death that brings
life to men."

II. THE ENERGIZING OF HUMAN NATURE.

What is the difference between regeneration and
the Baptism with the Holy Spirit? Inasmuch as we
shall discuss this more fully later we shall limit ourselves to one illustration. Deep under the ground lies
water, permanently abiding; in many places one sees
bubbling springs; from time to time showers of rain
fall from above. In other words, here are three move-
ments of water: water *dwelling deep within* the earth;
water *springing up* from the earth; water *falling upon*

the earth. The water under the ground pictures the indwelling of the Holy Spirit without which we cannot be saved. Rom. 8:9. The bubbling spring illustrates the welling up of the joy inspired by the Spirit. The water falling from above suggests the oncoming of the Holy Spirit to empower those already in relation with Christ.

III. THE GLORIFICATION OF HUMAN NATURE.

Eph. 1:13, 14 reads, "In whom ye also trusted, after that ye heard the word of truth, the gospel of your salvation: in whom also after that ye believed, ye were sealed with that holy Spirit of promise, which is the earnest of our inheritance until the redemption of the purchased possession, unto the praise of his glory."

The word "earnest" brings before us a custom familiar in Paul's day. A person plans to take a trip, let us say, to Ephesus. Approaching a driver he asks, "How much will you charge to take me to the city of Ephesus?" The driver answers, "Ten pieces of silver." He says, "Very well, I'll engage you. Here is one piece of silver as an *earnest*. You will receive the other nine when I arrive in the city." Now when the apostle describes the Holy Spirit as an earnest of our heavenly inheritance, he means, strange as it may sound, that no one on earth is fully saved. For Paul himself said, "Now is our salvation *nearer* than when we believed." Rom. 13:11. In other words, our salvation will be fully consummated at the coming of the Lord Jesus, who will transform our mortal bodies, so that both soul and body will be glorified. As a part payment of the fullness of our salvation, as an assurance and foretaste of the powers of the future life, we have been given the Holy Spirit. We speak about the fullness of the Spirit, but in the largest sense of the word we shall not receive the fullness of the Spirit un-

til we reach the perfect heavenly state. "It doth not
yet appear what we shall be: but we know that, when he
shall appear, we shall be like him; for we shall see him
as he is." 1 John 3:2. In that day shall be completely
fulfilled Paul's prayer that we may be filled "with all
the fulness of God." Eph. 3:19.

Dr. Swete, an English scholar, has beautifully described the future ministry of the Spirit in the following words:

"They shall hunger no more, neither thirst any more,
neither shall the sun strike upon them, nor any heat; for the
Lamb which is in the midst of the throne shall be their
shepherd, and shall guide them unto fountains of waters of
life." Rev. 7:16, 17. The double plural suggests the indefinite
multiplication of the reservoirs of spiritual life which are opened to refresh us and finally to satisfy the thirst after God and
righteousness. The glorified Christ is represented as Himself
guiding the saints, as if He had taken into His own hands
again the work which had been committed to the Paraclete-
Spirit. Yet though the mission of the Paraclete as the vicar
of Jesus Christ has come to an end, He is seen to be still the
giver of spiritual life; if the Lamb now leads in person, He
leads to ever fresh supplies of the Spirit, fountains of waters
of life, means of grace hitherto unknown or inaccessible, but
open to those who are accounted worthy to attain to that world.
The same view of the Spirit's place in the life to come is given,
with slight differences, in the vision of the New Jerusalem.
"He shewed me a river of water of life, bright as crystal,
proceeding out of the throne of God and of the Lamb; . . .
on this side of the river and on that was the tree of life,
bearing twelve manner of fruits, yielding its fruit every month,
and the leaves of the tree were for the healing of the nations."

The River of Life is seen by St. John proceeding out of
the throne of God and of the Lamb. So he traces to its ulti-
mate source both the present temporal (dispensational) mission
of the Holy Spirit and His future work upon the spirits of the
just made perfect. The whole flood of life which will, world

without end, make glad the City of God, issues forth from the glorified humanity of the Incarnate Son. The throne on which He reigns with the eternal Father is the exhaustless fountain-head from which the Spirit will be forever poured into the hearts of the redeemed.

CHAPTER IV

THE REGENERATIVE WORK OF THE SPIRIT

The Spirit is called "holy" because His chief work is sanctification, or the transformation and reorganization of man's nature according to the divine pattern. This sanctifying work begins at conversion, is continued throughout the believer's life, and is completed at the coming of Christ, when the glorification of the body completes the transformation of human nature. If any should ask, What is the difference between being "born again" and being "sanctified," we should answer by asking, What is the difference between the birth of a child and its growth? Regeneration is the *crisis,* and speaks of spiritual life *begun;* sanctification (as it is commonly understood) is the *continuance,* and speaks of spiritual life *continued.*

We shall now consider that operation of the Holy Spirit by which the divine life enters human nature as a transforming power. This might be studied from five viewpoints: Scriptural, doctrinal, psychological, scientific, and practical.

I. SCRIPTURAL.

Let us notice how the Lord Jesus Himself taught this doctrine.

One day, in the city of Jerusalem, a group of Pharisees and elders of the synagogue wended their way to the temple, apparently engrossed in earnest conversation. Upon entering the temple they went immediately to one of the side rooms set apart for the discussion of religious subjects. They seated themselves around a table, and they began an earnest discussion. It was quite evident that these were not of the hypocritical class of Pharisees, but that they were men hungry for the truth. The first man said, "Brethren, I have been listening to the preaching of Jesus of Nazareth. I have never heard anything like it in Israel. It is unique! What power and authority are in His words! And those healings—we have never seen anything like them. Who is this man, anyway?" Another spoke up "I too, have been listening to His preaching, and I have been wondering whether God has sent a great prophet in our midst." The next speaker remarked, "A prophet? I am just wondering whether he can be the *Messiah!*" A fourth suggested: "Brethren, why not go and investigate Him? Let us interview Him and find out who He really is. Let us go together." "Perhaps that would be unwise," answered the leader; "it might create too much of a sensation. You must remember our position in the synagogue." Then came the suggestion, "Let us appoint Nicodemus a committee of one to investigate this preacher and find out who He is."

Is that in the Bible? Yes. "Rabbi, *we* know that thou art a teacher come from God." The personal pronoun "we" suggests that he represented a company of godly Pharisees. If you happen to be speaking to a Jew about Christianity he may ask, "If Jesus was the Messiah, how was it that some of our wise men did not recognize the fact" The answer is that some wise men *did* perceive the true nature of Jesus. They believed on Him, but because of their positions in the synagogue they were afraid to confess Him openly. See John 12: 42, 43.

Now we understand what probably led to Nicodemus' night visit to Jesus. You remember how he began. "We know that thou art a teacher come from God: for no man can do these miracles that thou doest, except God be with him." And you remember that Jesus ignored what he said, and replied, "Verily, verily, I say unto thee, Except a man be born again, he cannot see the kingdom of God." Why did He broach this subject so abruptly? Because Nicodemus' opening words were really a courteous introduction to a matter that was burdening his heart; and the Searcher of hearts, knowing his need, answered Nicodemus' heart rather than the words of his lips. Reading between the lines, we conclude that the following was the heart appeal of this Jewish scholar: "I am tired of the lifeless services of the synagogue. I am an elder in the synagogue, and so attend the services regularly; but I leave as hungry as I come. Alas, the glory has departed from Israel; there is no vision, and the people perish. Master, my soul is hungry and thirsty for reality! I know little concerning you personally, but your words have touched a deep place in my heart. Your miracles show that you are a God-sent Teacher. Master, I would like to join your company, and escape the spiritual wilderness in which I dwell."

This, I believe, is what the heart of Nicodemus was saying, and that is the reason the Lord Jesus spoke immediately of regeneration. He answered, in effect: "Nicodemus, you cannot join My company as one would join an organization. Whether you belong to My company or not depends on the quality of the life that you live; My cause is none other than the kingdom of God, and that you cannot enter without a spiritual change. I speak from experience (John 3:11), for I myself am indwelt and empowered by God's Spirit. To belong to My company, you must share to a certain extent My experience. Why do you gaze at Me in surprise as if I were preaching some novel and strange doctrine? Surely, as a teacher in Israel, you have read God's promise, through Ezekiel: 'Then will I sprinkle clean water upon you, and ye shall be clean. . . . I will put my Spirit within you, and cause you to walk in my statutes.' Well do you know that though Israel boasts of being the people of Jehovah and the children of Abraham, they are unclean and unfit for the kingdom of heaven. The prophet says that before Israel can enter the kingdom of Jehovah they must be 'born of water,' and they must be 'born of the Spirit'—they must be cleansed and revived. And what applies to the nation of Israel applies to you as an individual. You must be born again."

In order to get the full force of Jesus' answer, let us imagine Nicodemus asking, "Master, how can I get this experience?" "As Moses lifted up the serpent in the wilderness, even so must the Son of man be lifted up; that whosoever believeth in him should not perish, but have eternal life." In other words, "I, the Messiah, must die, that mankind might live."

Passing to the fourth chapter, we read of Jesus' dealings with a Samaritan woman. And what a contrast! On the one hand, we see a Jew; on the other hand, a Samaritan! The first is a highly respected member of society; the other, a social outcast. The one is a person of strictest morals; the other, a woman of sinful life. The first, a cultured teacher of Israel; the second, an illiterate woman of the lower classes. Yet, both have the same need—spiritual transformation for entrance into God's kingdom. And notice that He employs another form of expression to impress upon this woman the same need that He had impressed upon Nicodemus. Skillful Soul-winner that He was, He adapted His method to the person's need. To this world-weary, sin-sick woman the Master spoke of the new birth as the divine creation within the soul, of a well of heavenly water which should satisfy the soul's thirst for eternal life. He says in effect (4:13, 14): "The water in Jacob's well lies deep below the surface, lifeless and motionless. But the heavenly water that I impart, while indwelling the deep places of human nature, will not remain there; it will force its way to the surface, making its presence known to observers, and continuing its course until the life to come witnesses to the individual the fullness of its blessing."

Thus we find that the dominant thought in Jesus' message to both Nicodemus and the Samaritan woman is that the Messiah is the Giver of Life because He is the Giver of the Holy Spirit.

II. DOCTRINAL.

What is the new birth? Let us illustrate the re-creation of man by the creation of the first man. In Gen. 2:7 we read, "And the Lord God formed man from the dust of the ground." Picture the scene. God takes the dust of the ground and forms a body. There it lies, still and inanimate. Though it exists in the world and is surrounded by sunshine and beauty, it does not react to the world, because it has no life. It neither sees nor hears nor understands. But wait! God "breathed into his nostrils the breath of life, and man became a living soul." Then he reacted to the world, saw its beauties and heard its sounds.

The same Lord who gave life to that body gives life to the soul. It is written, "The first man Adam was made a living soul; the last Adam was made a quickening spirit." 1 Cor. 15:45. "And . . . he breathed on them, and saith unto them, Receive ye the Holy Ghost." John 20:22. "And you hath he quickened, who were dead in trespasses and sins." Eph. 2:1. Man's soul is indeed dead to the spiritual world which is so near to it. But when the Spirit of God animates man, he begins to react to that world and live in it. This explains the young convert's hunger for Christian fellowship, and his eager poring over the Bible.

If you will pardon a personal reference, I have in my possession a very tangible evidence of my own experience of the new birth. It is a Bible which was given to me shortly after my conversion. This book, which at one time had seemed uninteresting, later became to me a living book. The markings throughout the book in all the colors of the rainbow are a vivid evidence of the fact; for it was my custom in those days to mark every verse that especially impressed me. The *Bible* had not changed; *I* had changed.

Let us consider another picture of regeneration. Have you ever attended your own funeral? You look perplexed. Well, let me put the question in another way: Were you ever baptized by immersion? If so, then you have attended your own funeral, for in water baptism there is portrayed symbolically the convert's dying to the old life of sin, followed by his spiritual resurrection to live a new life of righteousness. In water baptism, when the minister immerses a convert he says in effect, "This man has died to the old life of sin. God has washed away all his sins." And when he raises him out of the water, he says in effect, "He has now been born again by the operation of the Holy Spirit, so that he has arisen from spiritual death to lead a new life of holiness."

III. PSYCHOLOGICAL.

All that we desire to indicate under this heading is the fact that the operation of the Spirit in the new birth is mysterious and is therefore beyond human observation. Nicodemus asked, "How can these things be?" He wanted to know the *how* of the matter. Jesus simply answered, *"Marvel* not that I said unto thee, Ye must be born again. The wind bloweth where it listeth, and thou hearest the sound thereof, but canst not tell whence it cometh, and whither it goeth: so is every one that is born of the Spirit." In other words, the movings of the wind are real to us, but they are mysterious. So it is with the moving of the Spirit upon human nature. The new birth is mysterious in its origin: "thou canst not tell *whence* it cometh." There is mystery connected with its consummation: we cannot tell *"whither* it goeth." As John declares: "Beloved, now are we the sons of God, and *it doth not yet appear* what we shall be." 1 John 3:2.

But mysterious as are the origins of spiritual life, there is no denying the reality of its manifestations. Some of our intellectuals vainly imagine that they can blot out God and spiritual experiences by looking wise and pronouncing the magic word, "psychological!" However, Professor William James, one of the outstanding psychologists of the last generation, concluded after a study of the experiences of the saints that the new birth was an objective reality. As Jesus told the Samaritan woman, the living water would dwell in the depths of the human spirit, yet it would spring up and so make its presence a fact of observation. He told Nicodemus that the operation of the Spirit upon human nature was as mysterious as the blowing of the wind; but that those invisible movings are real is implied in the words, "thou hearest the *sound* thereof." What is the "sound" whereby we may know that the Breath of God has been blown upon a human soul? Paul the apostle answers, "But the fruit of the Spirit is love, joy, peace, long-suffering, gentleness, goodness, faith, meekness, temperance." Gal. 5:22, 23.

If you will pardon another personal reference, this feature of regeneration may be illustrated from my own experience. My spiritual awakening came when I realized this is not the only world, but that outside and beyond me is the spiritual world where God lives. I endeavored to get in touch with that world, reading various books in my groping for truth. After attending a gospel mission for many months, praying, and reading the New Testament, I was led to believe that Jesus was the Messiah. Then something mysterious happened. One evening I was about to leave the mission, and was standing at the door. I turned to listen as the choir sang the invitation hymn. I was not praying, nor was I expecting any unusual visitation. Suddenly I was conscious of a strange influence coming over me, very quietly and gently, but very real. The sensation was pleasant, causing my lips and jaws to begin quivering. I did not understand it. Very much delighted I proceeded home. Not until I lay in my bed did I realize what had happened and become aware of the fact that I had been ushered into the realm of spiritual life. Why it should have occurred in that particular fashion, I do not know. "The wind bloweth where it listeth, and thou hearest the sound thereof, but canst not tell whence it cometh, and whither it goeth: so is every one that is born of the Spirit."

IV. SCIENTIFIC.

Jesus said to Nicodemus, "That which is born of flesh is flesh; and that which is born of the Spirit is spirit." In other words, human nature can produce only human nature, and no creature can rise beyond its own nature.

Jesus did not mean to say, "Nicodemus, I *could* let people into heaven as they are, if I wanted to, but I have simply decided that they must be changed." No, the words of Jesus imply that, according to the spiritual law, it is not possible for human nature to enter the spiritual kingdom unless it is transformed according to the likeness of God.

To illustrate. All existence may be divided into five kingdoms. The lowest is the *mineral* kingdom; above that is the *vegetable* kingdom; the kingdom still higher is the *animal* kingdom; the highest on earth is the *human* kingdom, and highest of all is the *kingdom of heaven.* It has been pointed out as a scientific fact that no creature or object can pass from a lower kingdom to a higher kingdom, unless higher life coming from above, reaches down and lifts it into a higher realm. Let us illustrate that. Here is a mineral; above it is the vegetable kingdom. Now, the mineral can never enter a higher kingdom unless the vegetable life comes down and takes hold of that mineral and lifts it into the vegetable kingdom. Except a mineral be born again, it cannot enter the kingdom of vegetables! Now we come to the vegetable kingdom—unconscious life; above it is the animal kingdom. Now a vegetable cannot enter a higher kingdom unless animal life reaches down and lifts vegetable life into the animal kingdom. Except a vegetable be born again, it cannot enter the kingdom of animals! Here is the kingdom of animals; above it is the kingdom of man. The same law is operative. An animal cannot enter the kingdom of mankind, unless human life reaches down, humanizes it, and lifts it into the higher kingdom.

To enlarge our thought may we illustrate in another way. One day Bossy kicks the milk over. Can you go to her with your Bible and say, "Bossy, you have been mean and lost your temper. Now the Bible says you must repent"? Bossy will look at you with her bleary, bovine stare and continue chewing the cud! She cannot understand what you are saying. She lives in a different kingdom, a different world.

We are thus reminded that the gulf between the kingdom of animals and the kingdom of man is impassable. Take the most intelligent ape in the world, and train it so that it acts almost like a human being; then take your Bible and attempt to teach it about God and heaven. Will you succeed? No. A monkey is an *animal* and belongs to the animal kingdom, while we belong to the human kingdom. On the other hand, you can take a person in this world belonging to the most degraded tribe, educate him, teach him to read and write, preach the gospel to him and lead him to God. Why? He belongs to the kingdom of man. An animal is an animal, and a man is a man. That is the reason I do not believe in evolution. Except an animal be born again by a miracle, it cannot enter the kingdom of man! As I understand my Bible, God has not promised to transform apes!

We continue our line of thought. Here is the kingdom of man, and above it, the kingdom of heaven. The same law applies. Except heavenly life reaches down and transforms him, man can never enter the kingdom of heaven. It is the mission of the Lord Jesus Christ to regenerate human nature. And as the Lord God breathed upon the body of the first man, and caused the inanimate form to come in contact with the physical world, so the Son of God breathes upon the dead souls of men, causing them to live spiritually and to come into contact with the spiritual world.

V. PRACTICAL.

What is the result of being born again? John says, "Behold what manner of love the Father hath bestowed upon us, that we should be called the sons of God." The result is adoption into the divine Family; and the Holy Spirit is given to us that, having been adopted, we may *feel* that we are the sons of God. Writes Paul, "Because ye are sons, God hath sent forth the Spirit of his Son into your hearts, crying, Abba, Father."

Many privileges are connected with sonship, one of the most important of which is the privilege of freedom. Moses was commissioned to take the following message to Pharaoh: "Thus saith the Lord, Israel is my son, even my firstborn: and I say unto thee, Let my son go, that he may serve me." Ex. 4:22, 23. Since Jehovah had adopted Israel as His national son, the next step was to liberate him from bondage, because freedom is the prerogative of the children of God. Our prerogative as the children of God is freedom—freedom from sin, freedom from fear—fear of tomorrow, fear of death, and fear of the future. This is well illustrated by an old, old story with which you are probably already familiar. We are told that a railroad employee noticed a man walking down the railroad track, carrying two heavy suitcases. Approaching him, he tapped him on the shoulder and said, "Can't you read the sign? It says, 'No Trespassing.'" The pedestrian looked at him indignantly, and pulled a piece of paper out of his pocket. "Look," he said, "ticket." And it was indeed a railroad ticket! The poor fellow, who was a foreigner, thought that buying a ticket gave to him the privilege of walking along the track. The employee smiled and said, "No, no! You can take this ticket, and you can *ride*." And that poor fellow was happy. This may sound humorous to us, but isn't it a picture of some children of God who are carrying burdens that God does not intend them to carry? Let us be mindful of our privileges as the children of God.

However, while rejoicing in our privileges, we must not forget the responsibility of sonship. "Do all things without murmurings and disputings: that ye may be blameless and harmless, the sons of God, without rebuke, in the midst of a crooked and perverse nation, among whom ye shine as lights in the world." Phil. 2:14, 15. "We know that whosoever is born of God sinneth not; but he that is begotten of God keepeth himself, and that wicked one toucheth him not." 1 John 5:18.

CHAPTER V

THE SANCTIFYING WORK OF THE SPIRIT

The Holy Spirit begins His work of sanctification in the innermost part of man's being—his spirit—and works from the inside out—from center to circumference. Having effected a radical change in the convert's nature, the Holy Spirit continues His transforming operations. After birth the child must grow; after the new birth the convert must grow in spiritual character.

Progressive Sanctification.

This progressive side of sanctification has been well stated and illustrated by Pastor Tophel.

In spite of many painful vicissitudes, in spite of divers alternations of victories and defeats, the march of the Spirit, if it is normal, is, on the whole, progressive. According to a beautiful figure used by Professor Godet, "Man is a vessel destined to receive God, a vessel which must be enlarged in proportion as it is filled, and filled in proportion as it is enlarged."

To what may I further compare this invading march, so as to make you thoroughly understand it? Have you noticed that of fire among coal? When a few lighted brands have been enclosed in the center, and, if I may so express it, in the heart of a heap of this black and coarse combustible, we soon notice little flames forcing their way with difficulty among the lumps that are still cold. Now these flames seem to be stifled, now they flare up, accompanied with dense smoke; now, victorious, they reappear in all their brightness. Meantime the fire slowly continues its progress. It goes from the center to the surface, attacks lump after lump, penetrating them all insensibly, until, finally, after a lapse of time, this entire mass, red, incandescent, glorious, sends out its warm and brilliant rays in every direction.

This is an imperfect figure of that action of the Spirit, which from the heart goes to the surface, from the interior to the exterior, from the seat of life to the manifestations of life, to the actions and to the words; at first allowing many things which are incompatible with His holy nature, then, little by little, attacking them one after another, one year these, another year those, going into all the details so thoroughly that, nothing being able to escape His influence, one day the entire man, glorified by the Spirit, will be resplendent with the life of God.

A Hindrance to Holiness

As the Spirit of God works in the deepest part of our nature, He encounters a hindrance, perhaps the greatest hindrance, to His work. It is known as the "flesh," or the "lower nature." Paul says, "Walk in the Spirit, and ye shall not fulfill the lust of the flesh. For the flesh lusteth against the Spirit, and the Spirit against the flesh: and these are contrary the one to the other: so that ye cannot do the things that ye would." Gal. 5:16, 17. In many other places (for example, Rom. 8:1-13) we read of that enemy, "the flesh," which will master the Christian unless he masters it.

What do we mean by "the flesh"? Not primarily the human body, which in itself is not sinful, although it may easily become the instrument of sin. The human body is of God's creation, and—as it comes from the hand of its Maker—is a beautiful and wonderful piece of work. To despise and malign the body is to cast suspicion upon God who made both body and soul. After all, the body is what the soul makes it. Wickedness must be in the mind and heart before it is reflected in the flesh. So Jesus taught. Matt. 15:19. It is the *heart* (which includes the *will*) that murders, steals, and commits adultery. Amputate the hands of a thief and a thief he still would be as long as the impulse to thievery remained. Neither does "flesh" refer to human nature as such, for in the beginning God declared everything "very good." By the flesh we mean human nature in its *fallen condition*, weakened and disorganized by the racial inheritance passed on from Adam, and enfeebled and perverted by deliberate acts of sin. In brief, the "flesh" represents unregenerate human nature, whose weaknesses are frequently excused with the indulgent words, "Well, it is just human nature, after all."

The Flesh and the Instincts

Some time ago when my little daughter broke her arm, X-ray pictures were made to ascertain the extent of the injury. In a similar manner let us now X-ray the "flesh" to discover in what manner it hinders the work of the Spirit. The diagnosis will reveal that the flesh represents the sum total of man's instincts, not as they first came from the hands of the Creator, but as they have been warped and rendered abnormal by sin. This warped and abnormal condition constitutes the hindrance to the Spirit's operations.

What are the instincts? They may be described as those driving forces of the personality with which the Creator has endowed us in order to fit us for our earthly existence. For man is a dual being: he has a material side to his nature, fitting him for the earthly life, as well as an immaterial part, fitting him for the life beyond the grave.

We are now to study these instincts in detail, limiting ourselves to five important ones.

The first is the instinct of *self-preservation,* which warns us of danger and enables us to care for ourselves. Second, the *acquisitive* (getting) instinct, which leads us to acquire the necessities for self-support. Third, the *food-seeking* instinct, an impulse that leads to the satisfying of natural hunger. Fourth, the *reproductive* instinct which brings about the perpetuation of the race. Fifth, the instinct of *dominance,* which leads to the exercise of that self-assertion necessitated by one's calling and responsibilities.

The record of man's endowment with these instincts by the Creator is found in the first two chapters of Genesis. The instinct of self-preservation is implied in the prohibition and warning, "But of the tree of the knowledge of good and evil, thou shalt not eat of it: for in the day that thou eatest thereof thou shalt surely die." The instinct of acquisition is apparent in Adam's receiving from the hand of God the beautiful garden of Eden. The food-seeking instinct is assumed in the words, "Behold, I have given you every herb bearing seed, which is upon the face of all the earth, and every tree, in which is the fruit of a tree yielding seed: to you it shall be for meat." The instinct of reproduction is referred to in the statements, "Male and female created he them. . . . And God blessed them, and God said unto them, Be fruitful, and multiply." The fifth instinct, dominance, is implied in the command, "Replenish the earth, and subdue it: and have dominion."

Now, by the "flesh" we mean these instincts as they have been perverted and abused by disobedience to God's laws; and it is this perversion of the instincts that constitutes *sin*. For example, selfishness, sensitiveness, jealousy, and anger are perversions of the instinct of self-preservation. Stealing and covetousness are perversions of the instinct of acquisition. "Thou shalt not steal," and "thou shalt not covet" mean, Thou shalt not pervert the instinct of acquisition. Gluttony is a perversion of the food-seeking instinct, and is therefore a sin. Impurity is a perversion of the instinct of reproduction. Tyranny, injustice and quarrelsomeness represent abuses of the instinct of dominance. Thus we see that sin is fundamentally the abuse or perversion of the forces with which God has endowed us. I do not say that it is *all* of sin, but fundamentally it is sin.

Someone may ask, "If sin is the perversion of the instincts, will not some people conclude that sin affects merely the earthly part of man's nature and not his soul?" This is not a merely speculative question for in the days of John the apostle there existed a sect who actually maintained the above-mentioned theory of sin. The doctrine of this sect was somewhat as follows: "Outward acts are in-different; they do not affect the soul. The essential thing is to possess illumination, to follow the light, for salvation is through the higher knowledge. Bodily acts that the spiritually immature call "sins" have no moral value, and therefore do not affect man's spiritual life." Jude had this class in mind when he referred to those who turned "the grace of our God into lasciviousness" (v. 4), that is, who twisted the gospel message to mean that as long as we *believe,* it does not matter so much what we *do.*

The presence of this sect gives us the background against which many of the stern statements in John's first epistle stand out clearer. For example, when John says (1:8, 10), "If we say that we have no sin, we deceive ourselves. . . . If we say that we have not sinned, we make him a liar, and his word is not in us," he means that if any man lives in open sin and denies that he has sinned on the principle that outward acts do not affect the soul, that man is a deceiver. Compare 1 John 1:5-7; 2:4, 9; 3:6; 5:18.

The Bible teaches that sin not only affects our standing with God, but also corrupts the soul. First, sin is an offense against God, for in the act of sinning one uses his God-given powers to dishonor Him. Second, the perversion of the instincts reacts against the soul, weakening the will, defiling the conscience, initiating and strengthening bad habits, and creating evils of dispo-sition. Paul catalogues the symptoms of this soul-crookedness (one Hebrew word for sin means literally "crookedness") in Gal. 5:19-21, "Now the works of the flesh are manifest, which are these: adultery, forni-cation, uncleanness, lasciviousness, idolatry, witchcraft, hatred, variance, emulations, wrath, strife, seditions, heresies, envyings, murders, drunkenness, revellings, and such like." Paul considers these so serious that he adds the words, "They which do such things shall not inherit the kingdom of God."

The Double Cure

The consciousness of the twofold effect of sin led the poet to write:

> "Be of sin the *double* cure
> Save me from its *guilt* and *power*."

Because sin is an offense against God, an atonement is required to remove the guilt and cleanse the conscience. The gospel provision is the blood of Jesus Christ. Since sin brings disease to the soul and disorder into man's being, a healing and corrective power is required. That power is provided in the inward operation of the Holy Spirit who straightens the warp and crookedness of our natures, and sets our life forces moving in the right direction. The results (fruit) are "love, joy, peace, longsuffering, gentleness, goodness, faith, meekness, temperance." Gal. 5:22, 23. In other words, the Holy Spirit makes us *righteous*, which word in the Hebrew means, literally, "straight." Sin is spiritual crookedness, righteousness is spiritual straightness.

Civil War

When the Holy Spirit encounters the resistance of the disordered instincts, the "flesh," or lower nature, there results the conflict described in the following words: "For the flesh lusteth against the Spirit, and the Spirit against the flesh: and these are contrary the one to the other: so that ye cannot do the things that ye would." Gal. 5:17. A similar struggle is pictured in Rom. 7:15-21, 24. There Paul says: "For that which I do I allow not: for what I would, that do I not; but what I hate, that do I. If then I do that which I would not, I consent unto the law that it is good. Now then it is no more I that do it, but sin that dwelleth in me. For I know that in me (that is, in my flesh), dwelleth no good thing: for to will is present with me; but how to perform that which is good I find not. For the good that I would I do not: but the evil which I would not, that I do. Now if I do that I would not, it is no more I that do it, but sin that dwelleth in me. I find then a law, that, when I would do good, evil is present with me. . . . O wretched man that I am! Who shall deliver me from the body of this death?" It is claimed that these last verses describe Paul's experience before his conversion. That is quite possible. However, we must remember, first, that the words are addressed to Christians; second, that they correctly describe many a Christian's conflict following conversion.

One writer has said, "Christ may have come to us and taken up His abode within us, perhaps driving out seven devils before taking possession, but at one unwary look or gesture, or as the consequence of one unholy thought flashing in the mind with the speed of light, Satan, ejected from the soul, but lurking ever nigh, may return and fiercely dispute the domination of the divine Guest of the soul, and before the demon is routed again, a man whose heart has been a battle field of fiends and angels, may feel that he has endured not only the blows of battle but the tortures of hell."

We shall now ascend a high mountain, figuratively speaking, and take a bird's-eye view of this civil war raging on the battle field of the soul. We shall follow its beginning, progress, and victorious conclusion.

In the beginning God made man's body from the dust, thus endowing him with a physical or lower nature; He then breathed into his nostrils the breath of life, thus imparting to him a higher nature connecting him with God. It was intended that there should be harmony in man's being, the body being subordinated to the soul; but sin disturbed the relationship, so that man has found himself divided with himself, self opposed to self in a civil war between the higher and lower natures. His lower nature, frail in itself, has rebelled against the higher and opened the gates of his being to the enemy. This earthly nature of man, weak in itself, warped by sin, and particularly susceptible to sin and temptation, is described as the "flesh."

The situation may be illustrated as follows: Two bands of soldiers are quartered in a house having two floors. One the ground floor is a company of cruel, drunken, brawling men, and above is a group of soldiers who are gentlemanly, courteous, humane, 'and well disciplined. Because of the efforts upstairs to maintain discipline and the attempts of those downstairs to break discipline there would be a terrible conflict and perfect pandemonium. This is a rather crude illustration of the conflict that often takes place between the higher and lower natures of an individual, causing him to cry out in despair, "O wretched man that I am! who shall deliver me from the body of this death?" Rom. 7:24.

How shall peace be brought about between the combatants in man's spiritual house? Let us continue the same illustration. The well-disciplined soldiers on the second floor call for help, and place the entire house in charge of a superior force. In like manner, when man's two natures are in conflict, his higher nature may call in the help of God's Spirit. That is what Paul meant when he said, "Walk in the Spirit, and ye shall not fulfill the lusts of the flesh." By an act of the will the person gathers all his faculties and surrenders them to the control of God, the supreme Ruler. In other words, he makes a complete consecration. He obeys the exhortation, "Present your bodies a living sacrifice, holy, acceptable unto God." Rom. 12:1. He learns by experience what is meant by the words, "yield yourselves unto God . . . and your members as instruments of righteousness unto God." Rom. 6:13.

The Victorious Life

But what if the lower nature, or the "flesh," reasserts itself after this act of consecration? That this may happen is implied in Christ's warning, "Watch and pray, that ye enter not into temptation: the spirit indeed is willing, but the flesh is weak." Matt. 26:41. The possibility is implied in Paul's repeated injunctions to "put to death the deeds of the body," "crucify the flesh," "put off the old man (old nature)." Indeed, the saintly apostle testified, "But I keep under my body, and bring it into subjection." 1 Cor. 9:27. The problem, then, is to keep the victory achieved by the act of consecration and to hold the territory wrested from the influence of the "strong man." Matt. 12:29.

The solution may be illustrated as follows:

Perhaps some of you, while traveling over a new highway, have caught glimpses from time to time of an old dirt road that served the public before the building of the concrete highway. Due to long neglect, the weeds have practically covered it, making it almost unrecognizable. To make sure that no careless driver misses the new road, the old road has been barricaded and a sign has been posted, "Road Closed." All this is a parable of sanctification. Before conversion the soul was traversed by roads, or grooves, ploughed by disobedience to God's laws, and over these paths our energies traveled to sinful destinations, the end of which is spiritual death. Rom. 6:23. Energies and faculties which were created to travel the paths of righteousness, leading to life, were perverted into paths of sin, leading to death. In the experience called regeneration, the Holy Spirit built new roads, so to speak, through the soul, so that all the powers of our being journeyed over those straight paths that lead to God and life.

But after conversion we become aware of the fact that some of the old paths remain and that our inclinations, like mischievous children, are stealthily moving into forbidden ways. At such times let us immediately barricade those roads, figuratively speaking, and post a sign "ROAD CLOSED," so that all our inclinations, thoughts, and energies will be safely kept in those nine beautiful roads created by the Holy Spirit —"love, joy, peace, longsuffering, gentleness, goodness, faith, meekness, temperance." Gal. 5:22, 23. We shall thus obey the command, "Thou shalt love the Lord thy God with *all* thy heart, and with *all* thy soul, and with *all* thy mind, and with *all* thy strength." As we resolutely keep the barricade before the old paths in the soul, these paths will become practically destroyed for lack of use. This is the truth implied in Paul's exhortation, "Put ye on the Lord Jesus Christ (cultivate Christlike character), and *make not provision for the flesh* (starve it out!), to fulfil the lusts (desires) thereof." Rom. 13:14.

"Single hearted service of God is not an easy business; it costs time and effort," writes Dr. Kirk. "It is as hard as a campaign against superior numbers (Luke 14:31), as slow and costly as building a tower (Luke 14:28), as painful as carrying the cross was to the Master." We would not want it otherwise, knowing as we do that worth-while things are costly. Sowing to the Spirit (Gal. 6:8) may often mean sowing in tears; but "they that sow in tears shall reap in joy" (Psalm 126:5), for "he that soweth to the Spirit shall of the Spirit reap life everlasting."

No plea of weakness need excuse anyone from the pursuit of the spiritual life, for as the Christian prayerfully sets himself to do the will of God, he will discover that God is co-operating with him through His Spirit. This divine co-operation we call *grace*.

CHAPTER VI

The Energizing Work of the Spirit

"But ye shall receive power, after that the Holy Ghost is come upon you: and ye shall be witnesses unto me."

We wish to call attention to four truths that may be deduced from these words.

First, the main feature of this promise of the Spirit is *power,* not regeneration.

Second, *the words were addressed to men already in intimate relationship with Christ.* They were men who had been sent out to preach, armed with spiritual power for the purpose (Matt. 10:1); to them it was said, "Your names are written in heaven" (Luke 10: 20); their moral condition was described in the words, "Now ye are clean through the word which I have spoken unto you" (John 15:3); their relationship to Christ was illustrated by the figure, "I am the vine, ye are the branches" (John 15:5); they had felt the breath of the risen Christ and heard Him say, "Receive ye the Holy Ghost." John 20:22.

Third, accompanying the fulfillment of this promise (Acts 1:8) were *supernatural manifestations* (Acts 2:1-4), the most important of which was miraculous utterances in other languages, which manifestation was an indication of the fact that the gift of inspired speech abode with the early church. This supernatural utterance as an accompaniment to the receiving of spiritual power is directly described in two other instances (Acts 10:44-46; 19:1-6) and strongly implied in another. Acts 8:14-19.

Fourth, this impartation is *described as a baptism.* Acts 1:5.

The above facts represent the "raw material" for an answer to the question: "What distinctive doctrine or practice distinguishes your denomination from others, especially from those whose teaching bears a very close resemblance to yours?" The answer may be framed in the following words: "We believe it to be the teaching of the New Testament that in addition and subsequent to conversion a believer may experience a baptism of power, whose initial oncoming is signalized by a miraculous utterance in a language never learned by the convert."

The above testimony has been challenged by many people of spirituality and intelligence, one of whose objections may be stated in the following words: "It is a fact that there are many Christians who have not spoken in other tongues and yet who know of the Holy Spirit in regenerating and sanctifying power. Rom. 5:5; 8:14, 16; 1 Cor. 6:19; Gal. 4:6; 1 John 3: 24; 4:13. It is also true that many Christian workers have experienced anointings of the Holy Spirit by which they have been enabled to win people to Christ and do other Christian work, and yet these have not spoken in other tongues. In view of all these facts, what is there different and additional in the experience you describe as the Baptism with the Holy Spirit?"

We must acknowledge that this is a perfectly fair challenge, and one which should be squarely met if we are going to justify our existence as a separate denomination. To that task we now set ourselves.

There is one Holy Spirit, but many operations of that Spirit, just as there is one electricity but many operations of that electricity. The same electricity propels street cars, lights our houses, operates refrigerators, and performs many other tasks. In like manner, the one Spirit regenerates, sanctifies, energizes, illumines, and imparts special gifts. This variety of operation is beautifully set forth in the many symbols employed in the Scriptures to picture the work of the Holy Spirit. He is the gentle *dove* who broods over us; the *wind* which blows over us in cooling and life-giving power; the *fire* that warms and purifies; the *water* that quenches spiritual thirst, cleanses our lives, and makes us fruitful; the *seal* that preserves us and assures us of our sonship; the *oil* that speaks of usefulness, fruitfulness, beauty and perennial life.

The Spirit regenerates human nature in the crisis of conversion, and then, as the Spirit of holiness within, produces the "fruit of the Spirit," the distinctive features of Christian character. At times, believers make a special consecration, and receive that uplift to a higher spiritual plane, and consequent accession of joy and peace, which has sometimes been labeled "sanctification" or a "second definite work of grace."

But in addition to these operations of the Holy Spirit, there is another, having for its special purpose the *energizing* of human nature for special service for God, and issuing in an outward expression of a supernatural character. In a general way, Paul refers to this outward expression as "the manifestation of the Spirit" (1 Cor. 12:7), perhaps in contrast to the quiet and secret operations of the Spirit. In the New Testament this experience is designated by such expressions as falling upon, coming upon, being poured out, being filled with, which expressions convey the thought of suddenness and supernaturalness. All these terms are connected with the experience known as the Baptism with the Holy Spirit. Acts 1:5.

The operation of the Spirit described by these terms is so distinct from His quiet and ordinary manifestations that scholars have coined a word to describe it. That word is "charismatic," from a Greek word frequently used to designate a special impartation of spiritual power. Even scholars of the liberal school acknowledge that the book of Acts records extraordinary operations of the Spirit followed by outward expressions of a spectacular and supernatural character. In the words of one of these men: "The Spirit's work was conceived of as transcendent, miraculous, and charismatic. The power of the Holy Ghost was a power coming from without, producing extraordinary effects that could arrest the attention of even a profane eye like that of Simon the sorcerer." While acknowledging that the early Christians believed also in the sanctifying operations of the Spirit (he cites Acts 16:14), and His inspiring of faith, hope and love within people, this scholar concludes that "the gift of the Holy Spirit came to mean . . . the power to speak ecstatically, and to prophesy enthusiastically, and to heal the sick by a word of prayer." The point we desire to emphasize is the following: the Baptism with the Holy Spirit, which is a baptism of power, is charismatic in character, judging from the descriptions of the results of the impartation.

Now while freely admitting that Christians have been born of the Spirit, and workers anointed with the Spirit, we maintain that *not all Christians have experienced the charismatic operation of the Spirit,* followed by a sudden, supernatural utterance.

How do we know when a person receives the charismatic impartation of the Holy Spirit? In other words, what is the evidence that one has experienced the Baptism with the Holy Spirit? The question cannot be decided from the four *Gospels,* because they contain prophecies of the coming of the Spirit, and a prophecy is made perfectly clear only by fulfilment; neither can it be settled by the *Epistles,* for they are largely pastoral instructions addressed to established churches where the power of the Spirit with outward manifestations was considered the normal experience of every Christian. It is therefore evident that the matter must be settled by the book of *Acts* which records many instances of people's receiving the Baptism with the Spirit, and describes the results that followed. We grant that in *every* case mentioned in the book of Acts, the results of the impartation are not recorded; but where the results *are* described *there is always an immediate, supernatural, outward expression, convincing not only the receiver but the people listening to him, that a divine power is controlling the person; and in every case there is an ecstatic speaking in a language that the person has never learned.*

How may one receive this baptism of power?

First, *a right attitude is essential.* The first group who experienced the oncoming of the Holy Spirit "continued with one accord in prayer and supplication" (Acts 1:14), and naturally were in an attitude of expectancy inspired by their Master's promise.

Second, the receiving of the gift of the Holy Spirit subsequent to conversion is connected with *the prayers of Christian workers.* The writer of Acts thus describes the experiences of the Samaritan converts who had already believed and had been baptized: "Who, when they (Peter and John) were come down, prayed for them, that they might receive the Holy Ghost. . . . Then laid they their hands on them, and they received the Holy Ghost." Acts 8:15, 17.

Third, the receiving of spiritual power is connected with the *united prayers of the church.* After the Christians of the church at Jerusalem had prayed for boldness to preach the Word, "the place was shaken where they were assembled together; and they were all filled with the Holy Ghost." Acts 4:31.

Fourth, the effusion *may come spontaneously,* without prayer or any other effort, as was the case of those in the house of Cornelius, whose hearts had already been purified by faith. Acts 10:44; 15:9.

Fifth, since this baptism of power is *described as a gift* (Acts 10:45), the believer may plead before the throne of grace, the promise of Jesus: "If ye then, being evil, know how to give good gifts unto your children: how much more shall your heavenly Father give the Holy Spirit to them that ask him?" Luke 11:13.

But after all is said concerning the correct mode of receiving the power of the Spirit, it must be remembered that it is even more important to *remain* filled with the Spirit. We are reminded that there are three phases of the experience known as the filling of the Spirit. First, there is the *initial infilling* when a person is for the first time baptized with the Holy Spirit. Second, there is the *habitual condition* referred to in the words, "full of the Holy Ghost" (Acts 6:3; 7:55; 11:24), which words describe the daily life of a spiritual person, or one whose character reveals "the fruit of the Spirit." Third, there are fillings or *anointings for special occasions*. Paul was filled with the Holy Spirit after his conversion, but in Acts 13:9 we learn that God gave him a special enduement wherewith to resist the evil power of a sorcerer. Peter was filled with the Spirit on the day of Pentecost, but God granted a special anointing when he stood before the Jewish council. Acts 4:8. The disciples had received the infilling or Baptism with the Spirit on the day of Pentecost, but in answer to prayer God gave them a special enduement to fortify them against the opposition of the Jewish leaders. Acts 4:31. As the late F. B. Meyer once said, "You may be a man full of the Holy Ghost in your family, but, before entering the pulpit be sure that you are especially equipped by a new reception of the Holy Ghost."

Being filled with the Spirit is more than a privilege; it is a duty. "Be filled with the Spirit." Eph. 5:18.

CPSIA information can be obtained
at www.ICGtesting.com
Printed in the USA
BVHW011154310522
638520BV00011B/73